"In wildness is the
preservation of
the world."

– Henry David Thoreau

Contents

Can we be real?

I might be one of the worst facilitation students out there.

I dropped out of the most recent virtual facilitation course I participated in, after session three of eight. The last straw was when the instructor performed the macarena live on camera during the session. I just took my headphones out, shook my head, minimized the screen, and started drafting my goodbye letter.

One of the last times I attended in-person facilitation training, I left the class after lunch on day three and put on an absurd, aggravating, hour-long 90s-music mashup that is purely for novelty listening. I spent the entire lunch hour blasting this nonsense into my ears, trying to recover from the frustration I felt pent up inside the classroom. Better to be deluged by irritating, grating, tortuous music loops than to be trapped in a condescending learning environment.

Participating in facilitation training exhausts me.

Like, drains-my-tank-to-absolute-desolate-emptiness. There's a picture my classmates took in another learning experience: I have lodged myself lengthwise onto the tiny bottom shelf of a bookcase in order to achieve full-body compression and silence, in order to recover from the overstimulation of being forced by a facilitator to move through an overly-regimented pace of activities.

Occasionally, I wonder—is it just me? There are factors I've experienced that make this kind of thing hard for me. I was homeschooled for my foundational years, so if it's not a self-propelled, hands-on, quiet, project-based learning experience, I react as if I'm being forced to stand inside a walk-in refrigerator with an active lawnmower. I'm clawing the walls to get out, even without the macarena.

The thing is, I happen to be a very good facilitator.

This is partly due to the same set of factors that makes group activities hard. I learned from a young age that the quicker I could read a room, the more likely it was that I wouldn't be ostracized or mistreated. Thus, I built strong spidey senses without even knowing it: adapting to survive in overwhelming social situations by quickly making sense of a situation, finding a role to play, and creating meaningful connections. (In grade 11, as a guest to a district-wide student ambassador meet-up, I was accidentally elected President thanks to overly-effective lunch-break socialization. I politely resigned once I realized that it involved Actual Duties.) This baseline of empathy and sensitivity is the backbone of facilitation: a skill that has enabled me to improvise my way through uncomfortable, challenging, and surprising facilitation situations over the past twenty years.

Through this work, I began to see that the power of the collective is massive. There is more genius and possibility that gets unlocked when we choose to share our intelligence then when we keep our notions separate.

And I began to see (as you likely see too) that the problems we're facing in our organizations—and our society at large—won't be solved by ones, or ones-and-zeroes. Solo individuals individually geniusing won't be the way we move through crisis. And even the brightest AI engine (and I'm a huge fan) won't be able to fuse the creative and spiritual energy of a community to draw out a shared possibility. That work is uniquely set aside for groups, consciously participating in collective creativity. That's the work facilitation enables.

Sadly, it would seem that the only way we can meaningfully move forward is by learning to work together. I say "sadly" because this ain't easy. And I'm starting to understand I'm not the only one who feels that way.

Learning it isn't easy. Facilitation training tends towards the pedantic, and few of us have the patience for that.

Doing it isn't easy. Facilitation practice asks the facilitator to function as a sieve or colander: receiving everything people throw at you, maintaining firm boundaries, retaining what's useful, and letting go of what doesn't serve. That kind of function is, by definition, draining.

Yet, I really believe we need to learn these skills. Not in a stilted or scripted manner that denies our personhood and paints over it with a veneer of zestiness. We need to learn facilitation in a way that fully embraces the unpredictability, humanity, and wildness of the act itself. And we need to know how to work in a trauma-informed, sensitive manner as facilitators.

There is a semi-spiritual aspect to this idea. Henri Nouewn calls it the "wounded healer": the idea that at the place of our greatest weakness lies the lessons we need to learn—and to teach.

Facilitation has brought me face-to-face with my own limitations, challenged the stories my ego tells me, and propelled me forward into a process of unlearning that has helped me find myself.

It has the potential to take you there, too.

I hope that this resource helps to open the door to your unique learning experience, by offering some authentic stories of the failures, walls, curveballs, obstacles, challenges, breakthroughs, and flops that can be found in the world of facilitation. These true stories illuminate alternative ways forward. It's the book I wish I had the chance to read when I was getting a start.

As facilitators, we don't need to tax our personal energy and patience to the point of total depletion; we can take our own needs into account.

We don't need to attempt this art from a place of survival, where our existence depends on our ability to read the room; we can ensure we are safe and cared for.

We can recognize that facilitation is a crucial way to move through complex situations, without elevating the art to life-or-death stakes.

If you—like me—need a companion on this journey who helps acknowledge your humanity, protect your energy, and do the good work of facilitation without feeling like it's an epic drama, I'm hoping these stories can help. I'd like to offer you a different way to learn this craft.

A few promises:
1. **I respect your intelligence.** I believe you are a smart person, who can learn well, figure things out on their own, read widely, and make up their own mind. I will try to not be pedantic or condescending.

2. **I won't do the macarena.** There's a place for fun and games and humour, but you are here to learn, and you're bringing intentionality. So will I.

3. **It's going to be self-paced.** Move through this at the pace that works for you.

4. **We're going to use stories.** There are enough practices, principles, rules, agendas, activities, workbooks, playbooks, guides, and steps you can follow. Again, read those. But you need to learn from failure, from stories. And if you're going to spend time reading, let's get you into stories from the brink of catastrophe.

5. **Please get practice.** Embarrass yourself. Facilitation isn't safe. You gotta make mistakes and have major flops. The work of facilitation can't be done through books and video learning alone.

Ready? Let's begin.

Phase 1

Discovery & readiness

An effective session begins long before you gather; the journey starts with some intentional steps to more deeply understand your context and participants (including yourself).

Calamity in California

For a couple of Canadians, a wintertime work trip to California was a welcome idea. So when my former boss and I were asked to help facilitate a two-day workshop with a higher education institution in Los Angeles County a number of years ago, it was an easy yes.

Our client, Sam, had insisted that co-creative workshops to help the school's leaders arrive at a shared understanding of their future vision would be perfect for this moment in time. And while the client's supposed readiness, the balmy weather, and the iconic palm trees felt like an oasis as we started the trip—it turned out to be no vacation at all.

The first day's sessions, focused on purpose and vision, were with the organization's senior leaders: the president, members of the board and cabinet, and other leadership team members. We were exploring the underlying "why" of the institution. A high-powered room, no doubt, with a clear vision. But clue after clue began emerging that suggested no one in the room was aligned, interested, or ready for this type of co-creation.

The first hint was both a metaphor and an inconvenience—the room selected for us was actually a classroom, with rows upon rows of desks facing the front. We got to work before the participants arrived, sweating and grunting as we shoved tables aside and arranged leftover wheeling chairs in a rough circle in the middle of the room. We created the space for a series of activities that would connect people in the room, and spur people's imagination towards a future where a new vision was shared. Then the second hint came. One of the board members—a well-spoken young man, sporting a well-tailored suit, and trailing a tail of credentials behind him—interrupted a reframing exercise with an objection. "I don't see the point of any of this," he complained. "We're just going to imagine our problems magically don't exist any more?"

"Not...quite," I attempted to explain. "The work of developing a vision asks us to look past what's immediately in our way, to imagine what could be." I sensed from his irritated head-shake that he wasn't buying any of it.

The third hint was when the President excused himself before lunch, and didn't return.

That evening, my boss and I dined on an outdoor patio with our contact Sam and *his* boss, Bernie: a loud man whose booming opinions unfurled through the air.

"And that's when I stood up, in the middle of the whole assembly," he declared, mid-stride in a story, "and looked right at the President and said, 'This whole *creating safe spaces for people* has gone too far!' And I walked right out. Didn't come back. Quit my job that day. And called Sam here," he gestured at our client, who was nodding deferentially while also seeming to squirm, "and asked if he wanted a new job. And that's why we're here, now, at this new school, starting again."

As if on cue, a large pick-up growled as it rounded the corner behind him, a large flag flapping from the cab as the driver gunned the engines and tore down the street. I exchanged looks with my boss across the table and thought to myself: "Are we going to be alright?" We had landed in the middle of an environment that I was rapidly realizing we were not prepared for.

During the second day, we worked with a smaller subset of folks who were not members of senior leadership, to explore how the organization's brand and vision might evolve faithfully over the next five years. In our closing circle on the second day, we went around the room with a final question: *What are you taking away from these sessions?*

Participants spoke up to offer thoughtful contributions like, "I'm grateful to be able to zoom out a bit to ask questions about what we're here for," and, "It's so helpful to work together and gain some new perspective."

And then it came time for Sam to speak, to bring it all home.

"Well," he said, and started with some kind words about the external facilitators. "But let's be real." A shadow of intensity darkened his face. "I'm not sure if all of us are even going to have jobs any more after this, unless things change. None of this work matters, unless we can actually do something about it."

The junior participants in the small circle looked down, and fidgeted with their hands. It seemed the air had suddenly been sucked out of the room.

"I just spoke with the President, and he's under tremendous pressure. And I appreciate that we need time for these bigger picture conversations. But frankly, there are budget cuts happening and I can see this department taking a huge hit in the coming year, and not all of us being here anymore, without concrete results. This meeting will have been a waste unless you all shape up."

This message was not on the agenda. Nor was it in line with the stated purpose of the "co-creative" sessions we had just facilitated.

And there we were, left holding the bag (or holding the space, as it were) for safe, authentic, vulnerable participant contributions, only for the workshop to be used to ambush staff into a threatening guilt-trip about low performance.

What do you say in a moment like that?

Or more importantly: how did we get here?

Begin with the end in mind

Let's rewind the clock. A little bit of time travel.

The question here isn't about what to say in a meeting when the project sponsor goes rogue and becomes threatening—it's how to avoid getting into that situation in the first place. In this context, we can see so many areas where these problems could have been caught long before we even stepped into the space.

1. Do a readiness assessment

What if we had run some early, simple diagnostics with our potential client and participants, even before writing a proposal or doing any discovery activities? This might have revealed some key elements of their approach to conflict, and their openness to dialogue-driven activities.

In her book *Holding Change*, adrienne maree brown opens with a series of tools and questions designed to help facilitators understand the culture in a group before the engagement even starts. We've adapted these to web form, with a few additional questions of our own, to help facilitators explore a client's reality before attempting to suggest a way forward (see "Resources & templates" at the close of this guide).

This assessment covers a few key areas:
- The current problem: how are folks currently seeing their reality?
- Time, patience and commitment: what can they invest in exploring this problem?
- The intangibles: assessing elements that define the group's way of working, from joy and connectedness, to how they share power and move through conflict.

Gaining an eyes-open understanding of these realities will help reveal the type of culture you're about to step into, resulting in fewer surprises around communication style, group vibe, orientation to power, and overall tone.

While the above assessment helps us get a sense of the culture (which can inform the upcoming work of session design), it is also a screening tool to help us understand if we're a good fit for (or are ready for) each other in the first place. Not every problem or organization needs or is ready for genuine facilitation. Surfacing insights like this can help us suggest other problem-solving approaches that could work better.

2. Conduct discovery step by step

Before our initial discovery call, our client had already decided what
he wanted: external consultants to create the space for conversations
he wanted to have. While we did work together before the sessions
to develop an agenda, it wasn't authentically linked to his—or his
organization's—need or purpose. Why not? A deeper discovery process
was skipped, in part due to the pressure being experienced by Sam in
his home organization.

What would it have looked like to ask healthy questions in order to gain
an understanding of what was going on under the surface?

Sam was caught between chaos and order. The swirl of ambiguity, and
uncertainty in his organizational reality prompted him to decide that
what he needed was *order*—to clamp down on that chaos with clear
planning and activities.

However, we both would have been wise to remember the words and
teaching of Dee Hock, who has written that there is a healthy blend
of chaos and order, where innovation takes place (Hock calls this the
"chaordic path"). A skilled facilitator keeps enough chaos present to
stay open to new ideas, and enough order present to move forward with
clarity.

We use Hock's "Chaordic Stepping Stones" as a discovery tool to help
us navigate this tenuous zone. Through this series of questions, the
facilitator can partner with the client to better understand what's
happening in their reality, and co-design activities to truly address more
than just the "presenting symptoms." The steps to this process are as
follows:

1. Explore the underlying **need**.
2. Establish a sense of **purpose**.

3. Created a shared sense of **principles**.
4. Explore the question of **people**.
5. Explore the organizing **concept**.
6. Open the door to exploring **limiting beliefs**.
7. Explore the **structure** needed.
8. Explore how you'd like to enable a longer-term, sustainable **practice**.
9. Plan for the **harvest**.

It's not as straightforward as plowing through these nine bullets and declaring discovery done. However, you can use these starting points to create the space in an authentic interview or conversation. This type of dialogue can build a shared understanding. We've created a guide to the Chaordic Stepping Stones, deepening the steps with learning we've gleaned, to help with your facilitation discovery work. You can find it in the "Resources & templates" section at the close of this guide.

3. Explore your own needs and healing journey

I can still recall the way Sam's energy radiated over the phone in our initial discovery call. He possessed an urgency that made me sit up and lean forward, activating my desire to help. His ability to persuade meant that I was already saying yes, before I had even understood the ask. While I recall pressing in a couple times to ask, "Are you sure the group is ready for co-creation?" it was only met with insistence that the answer was yes. What Sam was experiencing was desperation, leading him to call folks he perceived as rescuers—from outside his country, no less. He was hoping that an external entity would be his ideal crowbar for smashing through his organizational distress.

This intensity caused me to shortcut a more healthy discovery process, seeking instead to step in to address the perceived need. My own desire to please was so active here, I barely even noticed the gap.

What was going on for me that I would willingly travel to a different country, offer my services to people who disrespected me, compromise my own principles and professionalism, without any questions? This is where the inner work of becoming a facilitator matters. Without the self-awareness and boundaries that enable grounded, healthy decision-making, we end up unconsciously supporting unhealthy patterns in ourselves and others.

What does it take to cultivate a sense of self-awareness as a facilitator? For me, it has been a journey to recognize when I'm reacting in survival mode, and to learn how to instead shift towards acting in a manner that is integrated, whole, and healthy. This inner work continues to be a life-long practice and process.

The work is a unique pathway for each of us, and can't be prescribed or copy-and-pasted; but finding support for your own journey can go a long way. That might look like counseling and therapy, coaching and peer support, journaling, mindfulness and embodiment practices, or the unique blend that works for you. These intentional investments help us explore and address themes and patterns in our self, relationships, and behaviour—which influence all aspects of our life.

Phase 2

Co-design

"Designing with the door open" is a purposeful practice that can significantly shift the outcomes of an engagement, by building trust and deeply engaging participants early on.

Stranded in the snow

An abundance of snow has cancelled my flight to a facilitation engagement twice now—both times causing last-minute stress and scramble. One instance led to awkward failure, and the other, to successful adaptation. What made the situations different?

The first time excess precipitation stranded me was on a trip to Nashville, Tennessee. My teammates and I had been invited to lead a day of in–person workshops that included (once again) a session with senior leadership, and a session with mid-level managers. We had created a loose plan for the day, but our intention was to rely heavily on in-the-moment adaptation. The goal was to sense the group's needs, and respond to what emerged—showcasing our live facilitation skills. I was the lead facilitator and my two teammates would offer support. The plan was safely stored in my head.

I had already boarded the plane when the announcement came that the flight was cancelled. I remember looking out the plane's rounded window at the blizzard conditions, watching the ground crews spray de-icing fluid across our plane while I talked quietly into my phone to explain the situation to my colleagues. The flakes whirled like a snow-globe—perhaps like the interior of my teammates' brains as they heard the news.

I would arrive mid-morning the next day, once the session was already well underway. But in the meantime, I would be on three different flights, through three different airports. This would give me enough time before my colleagues landed in Nashville to write, step-by-step, the whole plan for the workshop, so they could read it, learn it, and run it on their own.

I got to work, fingers flying furiously across the keyboard while the snow abated and my updated flights took me to stopover cities. Minute-by-minute, I explained a condensed version of the plan, logged on to airplane wifi, and shared it with my team before they hit the ground. They started the day independently, while I hustled from one more airport to one more taxi to finally arrive at the boardroom exactly in time for lunch, after the first session.

If you've ever had nightmares about arriving late and unprepared for an important meeting, this is that dream. An entire mahogany boardroom table was populated with men in suits who were staring at me, while I—the supposed lead facilitator—arrived half-a-day late in travel clothes, pulling a wheelie suitcase, apologetically mumbling, "Sorry I'm late."

When the session wrapped and we returned home, we received two pieces of feedback for our effort. The first was about our clothing: "Notice how the other gentlemen were wearing nice, pressed white button-up shirts." The second was, "We appreciated the work, but it felt a little too much like therapy. We would have appreciated more of a focus on the business side. Nothing personal."

The second winter whiteout happened on my way to a two-day event closer to home, within my own province. It was a high-profile gathering involving government ministers and a cross-Canada delegation of leaders in the youth mental health space, and I was to be the facilitator guiding the convening.

The announcement came while I was already through the security line and seated on the blue vinyl benches of the waiting room, blending into the noisy crowd of fellow passengers like Waldo. "We regret to inform you..." intoned a voice, rendering the din silent as anxious ears reached to hear flight numbers, "...this flight has been cancelled."

Groans and muttering filled up the waiting hall. I took a deep breath, and looked down at my laptop. In one tab, I had our session agenda, ready to go for tomorrow morning. In another, I began looking up alternative same-day flights. There were none.

It was time to call my client. They picked up as I exited security and moved towards the drafty doors where snow was descending outside. "I'm so sorry," I said, and explained the situation.

"Don't apologize," she responded. "It's not your fault. We've had a number of other delegates run into travel troubles on their way here— we'll figure this out."

We agreed that I'd try to rebook on the earliest flight the next day, and in the meantime the client would run the session without me.

How?

They had been involved in co-creating the agenda all along, and were intimately familiar with each minute of the plan—every twist and turn.

I tidied up my remaining notes, ensured they had all the access they needed, and arrived the next day, during the lunch break.

When I arrived at the hotel conference room, I walked into a diverse gathering of people socializing in groups at tables.

I saw my clients, and we greeted each other with a hug.

"We're so glad you're here!" they exclaimed.

"How did the morning go?" I asked.

"Great," they responded. "We made a small adjustment to one part of the agenda so it was a little more inclusive. But other than that, the plan worked great, and we're right on schedule."

"Can I just ask..." I said, looking at the client team, taking in their relaxed posture, calm faces, and unhurried movements, "seeing your body language, you seem genuinely calm and unrushed. I was sort of expecting a little more...panic? Has it really gone well?"

"Yes!" they assured me. "I mean, that was a little tiring, and we're happy we don't have to do the rest of the day, but the first part went just as we hoped."

I thanked them for their efforts standing in, and found my place at the front of the room to get ready to recommence the work after lunch.

Design with the door open

What shifted the balance between snow-day one and two? The difference was co-design.

In snow-scenario number one, we had approached the agenda in such a way that we wanted to "showcase our skills" to the client. This kind of "intention to impress" meant that a wall was erected from the start: the client was unable to speak into the design of the session. Thus, their judgment was reserved for the moment they were experiencing the session. And sure enough, judgment is what they brought.

In snow-scenario number two, the work started long before that phone call in the airport. We worked together through a full month of weekly planning meetings. The client group and I would meet to discuss what the agenda would look like, iterating bit-by-bit until we ensured together the purpose (learned through discovery) was linked with the activities. The activities were suggested and shaped in tandem. Not only did this mean the session reflected their *needs*, but it also meant our *relationship* was stronger, and their *familiarity* with the work was high. This meant that the snow wasn't a show-stopper. In an emergency, we simply passed the baton.

The work of "designing with the door open" means that the folks you're working with get the chance to offer their insight while it can still influence planning. It follows a saying common in the world of co-creation that originated with Barry Oshry: "Get involved early as a partner, not late as a judge."

What are the steps we might take to co-design sessions in a healthy, open manner?

1. Trust comes first

The clients who greeted me with hugs when I arrived late—this event wasn't my first time working with them. This was a client I had spent time with on another project, one which lasted the course of a year. During this time, we had shared stories of our lives and families. We had collaboratively and successfully delivered other meaningful work. We knew each other's needs and approach.

"Trust" isn't a button to press or a switch to flick: it's built and earned slowly, through layer after layer of shared experience. We don't always have this type of time when we are co-designing a facilitated experience in a client relationship. Are there ways to work towards building trust even within time constraints?

1. **Listening well.** In early discovery work, create a space where you can truly get to know the foundational needs of your client and the reality they're facing. There is a dual reward to the discovery process: yes, you gain information for your own work, but you also develop trust in an organic fashion.

2. **Connecting the work to purpose.** Synthesized well, the information you learn during the discovery process can provide you with a clear statement of the work's purpose. Equipped with a purpose, you have the opportunity to consistently bring participants back to the reason you are doing this work together. You can remind yourself and others what you're here to achieve. As you advocate for the group's cause and purpose, you will likely build trust: you are clearly on their team, pursuing the same goal.

3. **Mutual disclosure.** In a professional context, it can sometimes be uncomfortable to show our real selves. But the vulnerability of letting our armor down can reveal us to be genuine humans who are worthy of trust. In what ways might appropriate personal

disclosure help foster authentic connection with your engagement partners? As we relate to each other as humans in the world of work, we become more capable of doing great work together.

4. **Set some expectations.** You'll have done this if you went through the Chaordic Stepping Stones process, but there's no harm in revisiting it. How do you want to work together? If you can create a clear social contract that clarifies your shared values, style of communication, and the ways in which you want to partner, you can invite everyone to create the type of culture you desire in your relationship.

2. Thrash early

It costs less to change one's mind early in the process: it's cheap to iterate via verbal volleys and napkin sketches before anyone has committed to specific concepts. Better yet is doing this in close collaboration with those who have a stake in the matter.

The idea of "thrashing early" comes from Seth Godin. I like the word "thrash" because it implies a careless, helpless flailing—like losing balance or trying to tread water. It's not at all a posture of certainty or confidence. To thrash is to move wildly and unpredictably in order to find healthy footing. There's an all-over-the-place-ness to it that fits just right with the process of coming up with ideas.

1. **Make purpose visible.** If you ran through your discovery process well you've likely got a clear understanding of purpose. I like to bring that visibly to the surface at this point in the process—by either speaking it directly during a planning meeting, or writing a clear purpose statement at the top of a notes document.

2. **Choose your general direction.** Early on in co-design, there

are some broad-strokes decisions to make. What are you trying to achieve? I think of facilitation as happening in a few key categories:

    a. Design: generating new ideas and concepts

    b. Dialogue: creating space for conversation and discussion

    c. Decision-making: converging on an agreed-upon direction

Knowing your general category (or categories) of work will help you pick specific tools to choose (step 4).

3. **Share what you've seen.** Sharing stories with each other of experiences where similar work has taken place can help inform a new direction. "Have you ever been part of a great session that did this well?" By thinking through what another facilitator did well (or failed at), you can surface options that could be repurposed for your own work. Plus, sharing stories builds trust.

4. **Explore tools.** From icebreakers to ideation activities, a facilitator's toolkit is broad-ranging. You might already have a few resources that are your go-to's: favourite workflows or ideal activities. Or, you might find agendas and activities online. Continue to experiment with new activities, incorporate the ideas of others, and hone your own signature workflows. Co-design is a bit like a tetris game—figuring out where blocks of activities go and slotting them in.

5. **The rough flow.** You'll now have enough possible directions to create a rough menu of options and directions—and to form a loose layout of your plan. If you were planning a roadtrip, this would be your city-to-city itinerary. You're not yet choosing routes, accommodations or activities: rather, you are making a high-level sketch of where you'll go, and how long you'll spend there.

6. **Check-in.** Whether you generated a rough flow in a collaborative

session with your client or built it yourself, this is a crucial check-in point as co-design partners. It's the part where we ask: if we did this general flow of activities, do we think it would help us accomplish our overall aims?

7. **Share the invitation.** At this point, we may be at a spot where we can share or update the invitation for our participants. The moment participants first learn that a session is happening is the moment it begins. The first words they hear or read about the experience will colour their expectations and greatly shape how they show up. Take great care to set the table in a way that is linked with your purpose.

3. Fine-tune it

The work of fine-tuning an agenda design is something I didn't quite understand or master until the Covid-19 pandemic forced my hand. Before then—while facilitation was primarily in physical rooms—I could get away with facilitating from just the rough flow. I would rely on my ability to read rooms to navigate dexterously through the day's emerging needs, without committing to specific time-blocks.

This created a challenge, though: it was hard to co-facilitate with me. If the plan was only in my head, and if we were going to respond to what happens, how would we share responsibility for the agenda?

When facilitation shifted to become virtual, it became necessary to commit to clear timelines—which also enabled better collaboration with remote co-facilitators. It's now a pathway that I won't deviate from. (Our guide to online facilitation on page 47 gets into more of the details of digital work, but here's a version that applies no matter the medium).

1. **Sequence your blocks.** It's time to take our rough flow and put

it into a format that can track your time, and allow you to play with the order of events. After building these agendas for years in Google Docs—and manually updating the timestamps for every activity—I've now switched to SessionLab (where the extra work of adjusting times is entirely automated).

2. **Waiting, welcome, and opening words.** We don't always count this step among our "activities and tools," but how we arrive in the room and orient ourselves towards the work is a crucial starting point. I always design enough space for an arrival buffer, a meaningful Indigenous land acknowledgement, and a warm welcome into the space we're creating.

3. **Bio breaks.** What parts in the day will our bodies need to rest: to step outside, visit the facilities, or grab some food? These crucial moments of restoration make or break a session. I treat breaks as a moment to design around, and schedule them thoughtfully while I'm creating the agenda, rather than squeeze them in after the fact. (My rule of thumb is to aim for a 15 minute break every 90 minutes.)

4. **Down to the minute.** Playing with the time element requires growing our skill in the art of estimating. An activity, after all, doesn't start by magic: first, a facilitator needs to offer instructions. Then, receive any possible clarifying questions. Finally, commission the activity. How long do those moments take?

5. **Word by word.** This is particularly helpful if you are co-facilitating. I try to write down a suggested script to follow when providing the participants with instructions. Again, I have a tendency to improvise and speak extemporaneously (which I still reserve the right to do), but having a written record of what one

might say during a given moment can provide an anchor if I get slightly lost. It can also help pass the mic and share facilitation responsibilities much more easily.

6. **Who's got what?** Ideally, we're facilitating with a partner. With the agenda's words and timing locked down, it's time to assign responsibilities. Who's got which section? I try to aim for an equal balance between co-facilitators, but sometimes one facilitator is more familiar with the content or activity and should take the lead. Conversely, one of the facilitators may want the chance to try out a new skill. Often, it's ideal for the facilitator who speaks a question to also be the one to host the discussion and synthesize responses. Ultimately though, these are questions to explore together. As partners, discuss how to navigate the flow of who's hosting which parts.

7. **Now what's needed?** With a clear, fine-tuned agenda—down to the minute, word-by-word, noting who's got what—we can zoom out a little to ask if there's anything else needed. This might be AV considerations for a physical room, technical considerations for a virtual room, or conversations about note-taking, whiteboarding, screen sharing, host privileges, breakout rooms, and snacks. It's time to address any of those peripheral elements that help streamline the facilitation and enhance the participant experience.

Phase 3

Hosting & hearing

Hosting is all about attunement: finding a tone, listening with care, and showing up with authenticity and subtlety.

Bingo was his name-o

Before "facilitation" was ever a line of work I had considered, I found myself hosting a bingo night at my university's holiday event. Dressed up in formal wear that included a top hat, standing in a hotel ballroom, I spoke into the mic like a sports announcer. I would call a number with enthusiasm, and hassle the attendees to increase their volume of cheering. After several numbers my voice was already strained, and the awkwardness of my approach hit me. Bingo is a quiet game.

The epiphany was obvious, and I was slow to get it. Each time a number is called, the game invites just a simple sequence of actions: to review one's own card in solitary silence, and record the number if you are lucky enough to have it. Otherwise, everyone stays still and listens for the next number. Noises of celebration would be rare and eventual— coming from only one or two people, the first to reach their line of five.

I took off my silly hat and worked quickly to recalibrate the persona I had erroneously adopted.

Years later, I was invited to conduct some discovery activities with the leadership of a small local dairy operation. I was new in my role and career, but jumped in with gusto to ask questions and dig for answers with one of the senior leaders. Standing in a meeting room in a converted barn, I was exploring a line of inquiry to better understand her business, when she held up her hand and said, "Sorry, it's just…"

I wasn't sure if she needed a moment to think, or wanted to circle back to a previous question, but I paused.

"It's just," she continued, "you are so cute! Like a mascot, or a pet!"

This was not the interruption I expected.

I imagined myself dressed as an overstuffed sports mascot—perhaps a large robin's head in a striped baseball uniform, standing there in the boardroom, foam "#1" finger drooping to the table. Or a cute dog named Bingo, tail no longer wagging. In this context, there was no actual silly hat to take off, no mascot costume to remove, just me (and a slightly rude client) wondering: what could be different here about the way I'm doing this?

1. Find a tone that works

A quiet bingo game doesn't require a sports commentator's energy. An interview doesn't need a mascot's vibe. What *does* a facilitated room need?

So much of this depends on the room, and it depends on you, the facilitator, to be connected to your own style, and to be aware of the room's needs.

1. **The physical sound.** Like a magician scoping out a venue for

angles before the show starts, a facilitator should ideally get a read on the room's physical attributes before a session. This will tell you what type of voice and volume to expect to use. A smaller, carpeted room with few attendees will need something different than a cavernous, packed lecture hall.

2. **The content and theme.** What is the level of gravity or intensity of the subject matter you're facilitating? One topic might require you to find a speaking tone that is clear and assertive, and another, a tone which is subdued and calm. A situation requiring a large amount of sensitivity will ask you to find one path forward, as opposed to one with levity and lightness.

3. **The engagement needed.** What type of process are you facilitating? Fast-paced, dynamic activities will require a different energy than slower-paced discussion activities. It can help to match your tone to the tone that you're inviting participants to bring.

Facilitating is much like being a DJ. In fact, during some agenda designs, I actually create a playlist to go along with the activities. This is one way to consider what tone to set: what I choose for the waiting and welcome periods, what background music to play during quieter activity moments—it's all part of the experience.

4. **Ask your collaborators.** While you might have a sense of the room's tone, it's often helpful to do a "vibe-check" with your collaborators during the session to see if you're on the same page. That might look like asking, "I'm sensing the room's energy is waning, and we might need a bit of an infusion of movement or a break right now. Do you feel that too?"

5. **Simplify your questions and instructions.** I recall a session

I led early on in my career, where I gave the participants in a room *three different activities* to choose between on the screen at the *same time*. Each of the choices were completely new to the participants. This required them to quickly read each activity, make an uninformed choice on which one they want to try, and then do it. As you can imagine, the room froze, and that particular segment was an awkward flop.

We need our instructions to be as explicitly clear as possible. The objective is to spur participants on to…participate. This is the entire point. Your questions and instructions are the setup for the real work. Therefore, it's important to know what question you are going to ask, and what instruction you are going to give—clearly, and in advance. Don't let it get diluted with alternate phrasings or "you could…" possibilities that create confusion. Each time you give an instruction, you can ask: "Are those instructions clear? Does anybody need clarification?"

2. Listen like love

In our earlier success story, after the snowfall delayed my flight with my long-standing client, our two-day engagement went well. As we neared the end, I felt grateful. Not only had I actually arrived, but my husky voice and almost-sore throat had been supported by a microphone (instead of having to *pro-ject*), and my super-supportive business partner had sourced me lozenges, tea and instant soup for the breaks. In my mind, I had squeaked through by meeting the lowest bar: I was present, and my voice worked. Mission accomplished.

But afterwards, a participant came up to me to talk. "I'm a teacher," they said, "and I've done lots of facilitation. I thought I knew every trick in the book, but seeing you today…"

I gulped, ready for it.

"...that was the best facilitation I have ever seen. I realize now I have a lot to learn, and I'm going to be paying attention to what I saw you do today!"

I nearly choked on my lozenge.

"Thank you!" I exclaimed. "I'm genuinely grateful to hear that!" I didn't say this, but I was also genuinely surprised. Like I said, the bar I was trying to meet was, "Don't die."

I continued, "I was wondering if you could tell me specifically what it was you appreciated about my facilitation?"

(This is a gift I've adapted from the work of Marshall Rosenberg: recognizing that although they feel kind, a general compliment like this can be simply a judgment in disguise. To get value from a compliment, ask for what specific needs it met in the person voicing their appreciation. Rosenberg has great stories and examples on how to do this in his book, *Nonviolent Communication*.)

"Yes!" The person continued. "I really appreciated how you heard, affirmed and spoke back to the room what we said. It just felt like you were able to *hear* us."

I understood what he meant. That was the main service I was bringing to the gathering. I thanked him for his kind words.

If there was only one element to continue to practice, improve, and develop as a facilitator, it is the work of listening. Yes, listening means hearing—having your ears open for what gets spoken. But listening also means attending: processing and understanding what has been said, in the form of active listening.

As David W. Augsburger has said, "Being heard is so close to being loved that for the average person, they are almost indistinguishable." What you can offer as a tuned-in facilitator who listens well is the gift of helping a room of people know they have been heard. Often, that is the core need a community is carrying with them.

1. **Create the space for full statements to be made.** Though you may be tempted to cut folks off if they are taking up airtime (and that may sometimes be necessary), let participants have the time to fully respond to a question, and make their statement.

2. **Say thank you.** Every participant's contribution is a gift. It's the sole thing you were looking for when you opened the gathering. It's important to say thank you when a participant speaks.

3. **Check in with them.** After somebody has spoken, play around with your understanding of their meaning. Don't directly quote their exact words, but do rephrase and reach out: "Tell me if I've heard you right. It sounds like you're saying..."

4. **Try grouping multiple responses.** If you've heard a few folks speak, see if you notice any common threads between them. It could be an emotional tone (not spoken in the words), or a thematic element. Speaking it back to the room can be a helpful mirror to offer participants.

3. Host like a ghost

It was at a learning retreat called "Art of Hosting" that I first heard a teacher say, "If the participants thank you at the end of the session, you've done something wrong." The statement has haunted me ever since. How can a facilitator be *that* invisible?

If a facilitator has co-designed an agenda that truly puts participant contributions at the centre, it means those who were attending the workshop were the ones really sweating. While thanking a facilitator is certainly courteous (please do so), ideally a session has been hosted in such a way that it's clear the participants themselves have done the real work. How might we host this way?

1. **Redesign the room.** This might sound outrageous, but…the facilitator doesn't have to be at the front! It creates an immediate power imbalance, disempowering the participants and placing the host visibly in charge. Consider circles, stations or other ways to distribute the visual representation of power.

2. **We can move, people.** To stay sedentary and motionless is to give in to the gravitational pull of default desk-jobs. What about the "work" part of workshops? Connected to the above point, folks don't have to stay stationary.

3. **Equip participants to note-take and harvest.** Ready for another heresy? The facilitator doesn't need to personally vet and transcribe all notes. It's a little like holding other people's bingo dabbers for them. Aren't the participants capable of doing their own work? Isn't that the actual point and intention? It's important to think through how note-taking and harvesting will work beforehand, and to assign roles clearly.

4. **Reduce your own visibility.** Many activities a facilitator performs can actually be done in creative ways that don't centralize the individual leading the workshop. Instead of using your voice to call participants back from activities, try noisemakers like chimes. Instead of repeatedly speaking out the time, visible timers can

help keep everyone on track. Or try using written instructions instead of spoken instructions. In what other ways can you outsource jobs, in order to centralize your participant's purpose instead of yourself?

5. **Create breathing room.** With visible timers and a well-designed agenda, you'll be better equipped to not rush the room. While timing matters, so does pace and tone. A frenetic pace to cram in all the activities may undercut the breathing room a session needs for participants to think deeply.

4. Bring the authentic you

I was sitting in a sushi bar with a colleague in Seattle, after finishing a session with a university client. In the dim lighting, backed by black-painted walls, I asked my teammate if he had any feedback for me on how the session went.

"Yes, as a matter of fact, I have been meaning to pass along some feedback," he said. I waited anxiously for him to finish his bite of sushi, and wondered what it was going to be. Was the session poorly designed? Did I mis-speak at some point? Was it all a little too sentimental?

"This might just be me," he said, mouth finally clear, "being raised as an army brat and all that. But taking the time to press your shirt before you lead the room would be what I would suggest."

I blinked.

"Iron my shirt?" I asked.

"Yeah," he went on. "It was super wrinkly."

I wasn't sure what to make of this input. It wasn't about the facilitation. I supposed that was a good thing.

When we got back to our respective offices, the client sent over their own feedback. "It was clear you were so authentic and genuine in your work," they said. "We had heard from a different facilitator recently, and you could tell their heart wasn't really in it. It was just for show. But not only did you lead us to where we needed to go, we even remarked to ourselves afterwards, '*Did you see how wrinkly his shirt was*? This clearly wasn't about appearances for them. They really *cared*.'"

My teammate was unimpressed by my unpressed shirt, but it made an impression on my client. Talk about iron-ic.

I've since made adjustments based on this feedback. If I have to travel, I'm using the hotel iron. But it's also helped me realize that appearance in clothing ranks low on my priority list, and I'd rather continue to work virtually in comfortable clothes, where the relationships are strong and the purpose resonates.

We can dress up all we want, and even sound professional—but unless we are authentically engaged in our subject matter and people's needs, it won't matter at all. What does it take to find your purpose in your own work? Here's the work I do to connect the dots.

1. **When you can, get choosy.** This isn't always possible in spaces where decisions get made for you, instead of by you. But where autonomy exists, I try to say "yes" to projects, clients and moments that I'm truly aligned with. I want to be able to bring genuine interest and care to the cause I'm supporting. If I can't bring that, I likely won't be at my best as a facilitator, and it would be helpful for both parties to know that. What movements give you life? Be part of advancing those.

2. **Choose an intention.** Before commencing any gathering, I take a moment to find one word that articulates the intention I'm bringing. It might be something about what I want to learn, or what I hope to support in the work itself. If I'm hosting virtually, I'll write this down on my notepad or light a candle as a way of ritualizing it.

3. **Share that intention.** If I have a co-facilitator (and if we have a moment to spare before the session starts) I'll bring up my own intention, and ask them if they're comfortable enough to share theirs. It's pretty straightforward. I might say something like, "The word I'm bringing into this session is 'learning,' as I genuinely want to hear how they'll engage with the questions we've got today. What about you?"

4. **Release your own agenda.** The act of surrendering your own intentions for a session is a paradoxical choice. On one hand, we want to know what we're contributing. On the other hand, we are working in service of the participants' work, and in service of what might emerge. If I already have "the end in mind," I will be less equipped to stay open, nimble, and aware of new possibilities as they arise.

5. **Practice, and deepen your practice.** Relying on a script you've only seen once. Trying to remember details about a client you've only researched a little bit. Fumbling to recall how to perform basic technical tasks. These are avoidable foibles. I find it much easier to connect and commit to true presence when I have taken the time and effort to be comfortably familiar with the agenda, the client, and the work ahead.

6. **Accept what's present.** There is a now-ness to facilitating that asks you to only *be* there. To see who's in the room, to hear their

voices, and to take what comes. This cultivation of presence is almost a mindfulness meditation. It can be exhausting, and yet so empowering at the same time: it's the presence that people truly need.

And so, we've come full circle: all that discovery and co-design has given us what we need in order to be the most present to our task. We are able to connect with purpose, deepen our practice, and bring true presence to the room.

Facilitating a group of people through a truly purposeful process may be the true flow-state for communities: it's a demonstration of democracy—a visible interplay of interdependence. In creating the conditions for that mode of being, you are bringing peace and connectedness to the place where you work, which helps the world at large become more capable of harmony. It's worthy work.

Phase 4

Rest & recovery

Taking care of yourself *after* a session is an important aspect of a sustainable facilitation practice—one often learned through hard experience.

Feeling the stretch

I had recently completed a program in innovation and creative leadership, and was feeling absolutely inspired. Though it involved being away from my family (we had two young kids at the time), with four different one-week modules over the space of six months, I had learned new approaches to facilitation, built transformative relationships, and was inspired by big-picture ideas about change. I was positively pulsing with possibility, and I couldn't wait to share these ideas further.

As part of their marketing strategy, the company I worked with agreed to let me host a public training event, to help others learn these practices of collaborative innovation. The workload was less than ideal: I still needed to balance non-facilitation client commitments, didn't have any co-facilitators, and needed to travel while my partner was pregnant with our third child. But I was excited. My team and I found an ideal training venue (a yoga studio called "Stretch"), invited participants (we had 80 folks), and planned the event (an all-day workshop).

The night before, I arrived at my hotel room late and got to work refining the agenda and slides. Simultaneously, I worked on recording a celebratory song for my classmates in the program I had just completed. It was the wee hours of the morning when I wrapped up the work, and got into bed.

The yoga studio was colourful chaos the next day. Bright yellow walls and local artwork brought an inviting pop of colour. We quickly discovered the gaps in our plan. There was no water to offer guests; a colleague hopped in her car to acquire some. There was no exterior signage; we needed to improvise a sandwich board. Guests were arriving too early; they thought the morning was to start at 8:00 am (it was scheduled for 9:00).

When the event started and the first activity was called, the amicable atmosphere buzzed as participants got to know each other. To cut through the noise I climbed on a chair and...blew a harmonica I had brought. While charming, it lacked the volume to get folks' attention. Things were off to a challenging start.

During the Q&A after our day of learning, one person raised their hand to ask, "How is any of this different from conventional business strategy?"

I gave a defense of the value of empathy-driven, human-centric, collaborative innovation in reply, contrasting it with approaches that tend to favour data and analysis. I wasn't sure if I answered the question well, but it was enough to get a half-nod, and enough for me to wipe the sweat off my forehead.

(Yes, this is also the story where I offered participants their choice of three different activities at the same time, causing a stalemate of paralysis and confusion.)

We managed to stick the landing: the rest of the Q&A was thoughtful, great relationships were kindled, new tools were demonstrated, and the chaos mostly felt colourful. Survey feedback showed a range of reactions, mostly positive, with some constructive input to learn from.

It was an unreal feeling: I felt like we had pulled off something truly incredible. A complicated, all-day agenda, hosted in an interesting venue, with great participant energy. It was also rather exhausting!

But—as I've mentioned—at this time in my career, my daily work had not yet shifted to full-time facilitation. I still had many client commitments in the space of design and strategy for digital projects. And it just so happened that I had scheduled a meeting for myself to attend immediately after the session.

It was with the person who had asked the challenging question during the Q&A.

With the buzz of the workshop still in my ears, I joined two of my colleagues and our client at the coffee shop across the street, and we began working through the scheduled check-in. It quickly became clear we were not quite seeing eye-to-eye on a certain design decision.

I did my best to explain the rationale; they did their best to explain why it wouldn't work. A ping pong of increasing intensity ensued, as we continued to miss each other.

And that's when it happened: I lost it.

My hand slammed on the table as I gave an overly-assertive reply to a question.

We blinked at each other through the unexpected eruption, like a cherry bomb had just exploded.

And I realized I was at the end of what I could offer that day.

I excused myself from the coffee shop, leaving my colleagues to finish the conversation through the cloud of proverbial smoke.

Outside, tears were in my eyes as I reached my boss and explained the situation. "Do you need me to go back in there?" I asked.

As I asked the question, I was willing to do what was needed, but dreading that he'd reply with a yes.

What I notice now, is that I asked him what he needed. After overextending myself to the point of losing my composure, I was still making myself available to others instead of centering my own needs.

Thankfully, he wasn't the type of leader to exploit a person in a tough situation.

"Kev, we got this," he replied. "Just take care of yourself."

I called my wife to tell her the story. "I'm so sorry," she said. "Just come home."

Any thoughts of the all-day facilitated workshop were erased as I walked through the streets back to the office, ruminating on the experience of having yelled at a client for the first time in my career, wishing I could speed up time or teleport home.

As I walked in a daze, a simple line of graffiti caught my eye, black text on a white brick wall.

It read, "In wildness is the preservation of the world."

It bounced around inside me. In wildness is the preservation of the world.

This wildness—the wild, disorganized mess of this present experience. Something in there is key to how we'll move forward in full health.

How?

I think part of the "how" might be found in exploring what went on in this story, to identify what we can learn from it.

Spot the differences

There are so many elements to this story that demonstrate an uncalibrated approach to facilitation. I hope you'll already be able to catch most of them after reading this far. It's like a "spot the differences" puzzle. Here are the ones I can find:

1. **We need rest.** Before facilitation, we need rest. It's not okay to go into the session on an empty tank. In the last story, I'm away from home, lacking sleep, multitasking on a creative project the night before, and missing family. All of these elements are going against what it takes for me to be ready as a facilitator.

2. **We need support.** Working without a co-facilitator can be deadly. It's so much work to track with an agenda, read the room, and run a whole session; doing it alone is a very high risk. Especially in a situation like this, with 80 participants! My rule of thumb is to never fly solo. I always look for a co-facilitator, except for highly specific scenarios where one facilitator has been vetted as a safe

choice.

3. **We need recovery.** After a session, it's important to keep the decks completely cleared. I learned facilitation in an environment where most teammates were desk-based programmers and project workers; the concept of "work" was "time spent on tasks." This meant I often felt pressured to finish a facilitation job, and "get back to work." But facilitation is a significant expense of emotional energy. It requires time and space to recover. Pushing yourself to include an extra meeting afterwards is absolute nonsense. What needed to be scheduled was a nap, a walk, or a meal—but definitely not a meeting.

4. **We need...everything we already talked about in this guide.** Did you notice how I was still working on the agenda and slides the night before? Those need to be locked in long before, through co-design. My harmonica? I needed a noisemaker calibrated to the room's needs, along with all the event details. What about an event co-designed in advance, with partners, not discovered in a scurry on the morning-of? Without the steps this guide lays out, what we get is colourful chaos.

5. **We need love.** I can see it in the care my colleague offered me both in the workshop setup, and during the coffee-shop encounter. I can hear it from my supportive boss, and from my wife over the phone. This is a deep kind of care that can accommodate the chaos and still offer stability. We're growing, wild creatures, flailing about in uncertainty, but the anchor of love can help us travel through this ambiguous world and still arrive somewhat intact, and cared for.

It wasn't long after this experience that my third child was born and I took paternity leave to care for my family. Parental leave is not a rest (at all): it involves an all-encompassing emotional and physical bootcamp of all-nighters and all-dayers. But it was a change from work. It provided me with a purposeful pause to put down my professional tools, and pay attention to a different kind of wildness. This is the type of wildness where life emerges. *That's* the preservation of the world. Sometimes we need to walk away in order to get to where we need to go.

Online facilitation

Adapting our practices
for digital gatherings

How can you tell you're in the middle of a poorly-designed online workshop? It's the moment the meeting host asks a question, and expects people to just *come off mute and answer out loud.*

"Wait," you might be asking. "Isn't that every online meeting?"

It doesn't have to be.

Online workshops and meetings can be leagues ahead of in-person events—with the right hosting and process design.

A healthy online workshop can:
- create greater **psychological safety** for participants (by ensuring folks are in a comfortable home environment),
- let us hear from **introverts and extroverts** alike (by allowing time for processing and reflection),
- **reduce power differentials** and cognitive **biases** in the room (by welcoming input but anonymizing perspectives),
- record more **data** (many activities can be digitized and saved, including typed responses),
- reduce your **carbon footprint** (there's less travel involved),
- help people feel **heard and supported** (by seeing their own words reflected back to them),
- and create life-giving, enriching **sensory experiences** (by using music and sound cues well).

Remote working is familiar to most of us these days—but we still need to adapt. As we find ourselves and our organizations moving into a "new normal" after a series of global events, our practices for working together as part of virtually connected teams require evolution and sharpening.

What's so hard about running virtual gatherings?

When we ask our community of learners what's hard about online events, we hear a range of answers, including...

- **"Participants don't stay engaged."** They'll zone out, multitask, turn cameras off, or otherwise treat the meeting as if it's optional.
- **"'Zoom fatigue' is real."** The idea of yet-another-screen-mediated meeting is draining for many.
- **"It's hard to read the room."** In a virtual setting, it can be challenging to absorb non-verbal cues and detect shifts in body language.
- **"It can feel purposeless."** Without a clear anchor or mission, folks can feel adrift (and now we're back at the first problem).

There's no minimizing the real challenges of virtual meetings. But it's worth asking yourself: what if those blockers were addressed—would the virtual meeting still be a challenge? Let's say participants were more engaged than if we were in a physical room. Let's imagine our purpose is laser-focused. Let's imagine you were able to appropriately "read" the participants. Would that be worth your time?

As Harvard Business Review has published, "Extensive research shows that, when it comes to innovation, hybrid and remote teams can outcompete in-person teams."[1] You can design and lead the type of virtual meetings that respect the time and contribution of all participants—and achieve your purpose even more powerfully than in the past.

Something we often say about virtual sessions is, "You can't read the room, but you can lead the room." While collaborative planning is a

---

[1] *"Why Virtual Brainstorming Is Better for Innovation," hbr.org, 02/03/22*

differentiator for all facilitation efforts, virtual facilitation *demands* we plan and design our work together in advance—collaboratively, clearly, and in far more detail. This creates remarkable opportunities for the equitable inclusion of all voices. That's leading the room. It's a switch, but a very worthwhile one.

The three essential elements of better virtual meetings

When it comes to virtual facilitation, there are three main areas to pay attention to, in order to lead well.

1. **Plan with intention.** As we've seen already, the work starts well before we are in the "room" together.
2. **Orchestrate with precision.** Details matter more than ever in the digital space.
3. **Bring closure.** Ask for feedback and evolve the practice.

Adapting and adjusting

Consider this metaphor: if you've developed your skills as a cook over your lifetime, you likely have developed a few go-to recipes. There's perhaps a lovely gourmet dish that you might make if you're having guests—let's say it's a lasagne. It might take a while, and involve some prep and planning. You've invested the time to know which dishes you need, what ingredients to purchase, and the time it takes to get it right to really serve your guests well. That kind of hospitality and intentionality goes a long way—it takes skill, but more than that, it takes intention.

However, a lasagne isn't the meal you'll make on a rushed weekday evening. Sometimes, you just need to put together a quick pot of mac-and-cheese.

This is also true with online gatherings: sometimes you're going to choose the route that takes maximum prep and intention. And sometimes, it's just you and some familiar attendees, and you're here to get the job done quickly. That's the difference between a formal workshop and a lighter engagement, such as an online meeting. Having the skills to lead an in-depth workshop equips you to know what's appropriate to simplify for a straightforward online meeting. You gotta know the rules to break 'em. At the end of this section, you'll find a few tips to help you adapt these robust principles to suit various situations.

Online facilitation: Principle 1

Plan with intention

From purpose, to invitation, design, assigning roles, and tech selection—planning work is responsible for most of the experience you will ultimately deliver.

All good facilitation takes significant planning. With online facilitation, however, it's safe to say that 90% of the effort comes before you even step into the digital room. Your work in the up-front discovery, design and prep is absolutely key to your success in this type of engagement.

As before, establishing your purpose is key. This foundational piece remains the same. However, other elements of planning are going to require a slightly different perspective and more attention to detail.

Design for equity

One of the most powerful insights that has come out of our remote facilitation experience is the way it can enable a more equitable space for engagement when designed well.

Think about it: who typically speaks during in-person sessions? The extroverted personality, the person who is able to think quickly on the spot and speak eloquently to their ideas. But virtual engagements more easily create a healthy space for those with other strengths (like the introvert). They can participate in a way that is safe and meaningful.

To take advantage of this, you need to make design choices and use tools that allow for an intentional flow of personal reflection, digital capture, and then space for small or large group discussion. This helps facilitate participation in ways that we might never have considered before.

As you consider selecting the right activities for your virtual session, consider a flow that allows for the following:

- **Individual reflection:** give time for independent thinking to process and contribute to the work.
- **Breakout groups:** create smaller groupings of people for meaningful discussions that build on the personal reflection.
- **Full-group discussion:** design a large group format for wider processing and reflecting of the work done as individuals and small groups.

When you do this, you'll never have to ask that awkward question again: "Does anyone have any thoughts about this?" (That results in crickets.) You don't have to create a sense of disengagement and exclusion for any participants who may not have the level of comfort needed to unmute and speak to a virtual room of square-framed heads looking intently in their direction. Instead, you're creating an intentional flow to ask a question, invite reflection, foster discussion, and gather input.

An intentional agenda

In a virtual meeting, there's no such thing as low engagement—just a badly designed agenda. If the facilitator asks a question and nobody answers, that's the first sign of a poorly-designed meeting. But there's no need to let it get to that point. If you've created space for personal reflection, have a way to let people write out their thoughts, and a format for folks to meaningfully share their insights in a low-pressure way, you've already created the space for true engagement. And it starts when you design the agenda, not when you're in the room.

A well-designed agenda provides a minute-by-minute schedule for every activity, including instructions and breaks. Yes, down to the minute. Timing is everything. Breaking down activities—minutes to present, minutes to individually reflect, minutes for group discussion—will keep the session on-track. When the facilitation role is being shared by two or more people, this thoughtful orchestration becomes even more important. Clear articulation of ownership and timing ensures that the workshop flows as a seamless experience for the participants.

It's important to remember that digital fatigue is real, and building in 15-minute breaks every 90 minutes will make a world of difference to participants. Our experience suggests that participants begin to really tap out at the three-hour mark in digital contexts. Whereas we might run a full day (eight-hour) workshop in-person without hesitation, with online experiences we would consider breaking the session into two half-day sessions. The time between sessions can be thoughtfully guided; facilitators can leave participants with questions to consider before returning for the final portion of the experience.

Establish facilitators' roles

Just as we communicate a clear role and set of expectations to our participants in the invitation, so too we need to articulate the facilitator's role and what the participants can expect of them. This is particularly true when we have multiple facilitators sharing ownership of a digital gathering: we need to clarify how their roles intersect and flow between one another. We've found there are three facilitator roles that contribute to the success of a virtual session.

The Process Facilitator

This role remains somewhat fluid and adaptable between co-facilitators over the course of the workshop. As facilitators, we will often switch between content and technical modes as we shift between different activities. The variation in voice, tone, and style which different facilitators bring into the space can be refreshing for participants, and can help keep engagement high. The Process Facilitator in any given moment leads the overarching activities and content, whether that's delivering lecture-style content, or facilitating the group as they work and ideate together.

The Technical Facilitator

This role can also remain fluid between co-facilitators. Whoever is wearing this hat owns the flow of the digital space—managing participant chat threads and moving participants between different modes such as breakout groups and individual activities. This role instructs on logistics, and helps participants anticipate how to interact with each other in this "new" medium.

The Technical Producer

This role can perhaps be considered a "nice to have," though once we hit the 30+ participant mark, our experience has been that the role becomes mission critical. A technical producer is a silent, behind-the-scenes manager who facilitates the nitty-gritty details of the digital space. They may set up the technical platform that we'll be using to run a workshop, manage breakout rooms, support participant assignments, and tackle technical issues. They also tend to run a technical dress rehearsal. Often this role is performed by an IT support professional.

Select the technology

Choosing the right technology is generally the last step in our process— and with good reason. Our agenda should inform the software choice, not vice versa. The platforms we use will be informed by a few considerations:

- How many participants do we have?
- Is there a technology that participants and facilitators are already comfortable with, which also meets our agenda needs?
- What different modes of work do we need to accommodate? (ie. breakout rooms, screen sharing)
- Is the technology frictionless? (Requires no login or has a simple login. Presents a minimal learning curve.)

Currently, Zoom is our team's video platform of choice, largely due to its flexibility, interface, and specific, helpful features such as breakout rooms. We've found that most (if not all) folks have had some experience with this platform, and those who haven't tend to catch on quickly. Though Zoom (and most other platforms) accommodates any device (desktop, tablet, mobile), we've consistently found that participants engage best on a desktop device.

Consider how to deliver the collaborative activities that are likely part of your workshop flow. Whether it's shared Word docs, sticky notes, whiteboards, or an interactive spreadsheet—having a tool that is accessible for all participants and works in realtime is a key way to create a sense of togetherness and collaboration from afar. We've used Google Jamboard, Miro, and even Google Docs and Sheets with lots of success. Let your activities inform the technology choice that will serve you best.

In cases where you are introducing a tool that may be new to folks— let's take Miro as an example—ensure there is time for onboarding and familiarization with the tool ahead of the workshop. The goal of a tool is to facilitate the flow of the content, and you want to avoid it becoming a point of friction and frustration. Our team has created some test boards to help users try out the basic functions of Miro before they even get into the room, so participants can build confidence in their skills.

Online facilitation: Principle 2

Orchestrate with precision and presence

When it's time to gather, show up with intentionality, and model presence and engagement to welcome the group into a purposeful experience.

1. Set up your workspace for success

Practically, we like to ensure that our work space—the laptop and second monitor—are set up to ensure optimal viewing and flow. On the laptop, we will be running the video conferencing tool at full screen. This is where the webcam is, which means that the majority of our time as facilitators is spent looking attendees in the eye, and practicing presence. On the second monitor, we will have a browser window open for whatever collaboration tool we're using, as well as a separate browser window for the agenda that we're referencing. We will also have a backchannel chat running among co-facilitators (most often on Slack) in case we need to make any quick adjustments, or pass vital information to one another.

One note on the backchannel: we try to keep communication here to a minimum. We find that pauses to openly collaborate and temperature-check with a co-facilitator in the presence of participants is completely appropriate and builds confidence in the group. Often, if you as a facilitator are sensing that something is "off" or that you need to slightly reorient your plan, the participants are feeling it too. Naming these feelings and working through them in a collaborative way demonstrates the approach that you're aiming to cultivate amongst participants. That being said, sometimes you need a private connect with a co-facilitator, and the backchannel provides this route.

This image is a mock-up of how one of our facilitators sets up their workstation, on one large monitor:

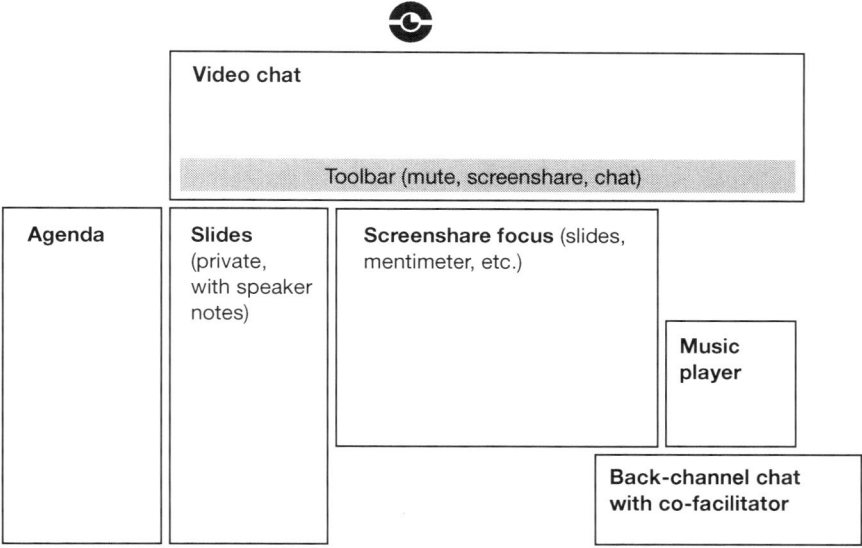

Digital defaults:
- All tabs closed
- Other apps closed
- *Do not disturb* on

Non-digital items:
- Water
- Notepad
- Headphones

- A quiet space
- Coffee?

2. Lead with presence

It's now finally time to deliver the workshop. Remember when we said 90% of the work was in the pre-planning? It's true. Once you step into the room, your job as the facilitator is to follow through on all the great plans that you have laid out in advance.

So much of your role at this moment is to set the tone, embodying the invitation for people to show up and engage. We find it helpful to be in the room at least ten minutes before the start time, with some fun and chill waiting tunes playing while participants trickle in.

Once participants have arrived and you begin the session—ideally on time—a simple way to establish the environment is by restating the invitation as to how we want participants to show up. Think of it as the workshop charter. Some invitations you might mention include:

- **Be present.** Turn off distractions (phones, tabs for internet browsing and email checking, other communication notifications).
- **Be on time.**
- **Turn on your camera** to create a sense of togetherness.
- **Be an active participant.** Our success is dependent on everyone engaging in the work.
- **Be conscious.** Hold space for all team members to contribute. Have an awareness of time, and share the space.

Asking attendees to give a head nod or a thumbs up to show their agreement and buy-in to this invitation helps to establish participation and engagement from the outset.

3. Model engagement

We've likely all experienced how easy it is to zone out on video conference calls. Body language is harder to read, subtle sounds and tone of voice can be missed, and we can struggle to feel truly connected to one another. A key requirement—and one that we would say is non-negotiable when running a workshop—is having all participants turn their cameras on. This makes a world of difference in cultivating togetherness.

We generally ask attendees to keep their mics muted when not speaking—it really helps to cut down on noise, and improves overall sound quality for everyone. However, as a facilitator, it helps to keep your mic unmuted and provide participants with nods and gentle affirmations when appropriate. These small indicators of engagement go a long way for participants who are sharing.

Another piece to consider with participants sharing in the group setting is how to phrase questions. Generally speaking, posing the question "does anybody have anything to say or contribute?" falls fairly flat as a facilitation method. Either you are met with radio silence, as no one wants to be the first to break the silence, or there are too many voices and not enough time to manage it well. Often we will intentionally call on specific people and ask for a contribution, particularly when we are working in small breakout groups. Preparing people for times of sharing, letting them know we'll be coming back to the full group session, and asking one spokesperson from each breakout group to share for two minutes, is a great way to set folks up for success.

As a facilitator in the digital space, you'll find yourself in moments where you are pausing and waiting, as the groups split off into their breakout rooms and you are playing the role of timekeeper and preparing for the next activity. In these moments, you have a great opportunity to connect with your co-facilitator, check in on how the session is running, and make any necessary adjustments to timing or activities. Additionally, you can stay present to respond to raised hands or calls for help from breakout groups where folks may be stuck. It might also be a quick opportunity to take a quick break and grab a coffee.

Online facilitation: Principle 3

Bring closure

Don't miss the opportunity to wrap up well; seek feedback to understand your participants' experience, and gather takeaways to ensure that insights and follow-up actions are well-defined.

1. Ask for feedback

One of our team's goals is to continuously learn and improve the workshops we offer. This is particularly true of digital engagements, as this is a new, experimental field for almost everyone. Every time we run a workshop, it's an opportunity to hone our skills, and become aware of our blindspots. What has "always worked" but might need to be rethought for a new context? Which tools resonate with specific groups of participants?

The easiest way to gain valuable feedback is to send a brief survey to participants following the workshop. We will generally share this in the video conferencing chat as part of our closing time, as well as send a link in a follow-up email to all participants. The key is to ask meaningful questions that will help your team identify areas for growth, while also keeping the survey short and easy to complete in a short amount of time.

2. Harvest takeaways

One of the greatest gifts of facilitating in the remote digital space is that the past work of transcribing paper notes to digital is already done for you. Be sure to leverage digital tools that will support your goals and make the synthesis process easier for you or your team.

Adapting the principles

Not every online meeting is an online workshop where all participants are on-screen. Here's tips for adapting these methods to hybrid gatherings, or meetings that call for lighter planning.

Need the minimalist approach?

To be honest, the first and best way to improve most virtual meetings is to cancel. (What?!) It's true: if your purpose is unclear, your participants don't want to be there, and you're too tired to lead well, just let it go. Reclaim the time. Don't force it. Go for a stroll. Please.

At the same time, if reading this guide causes you to feel a little paralyzed or unsure because of the seeming complexity of *doing this well*, we understand. We need not choose between all-or-nothing. There is no such thing as perfect facilitation. But we do want to encourage you to hold true to a few core principles in order to create the space for meaningful listening.

If your online meeting is more of a mac-and-cheese moment than a lasagne-feast, here's what not to skimp on:

- **Know your purpose.** If you can't articulate the reason for your meeting in one sentence or less, cancel it.

- **Have a clear invitation.** Help attendees know the reasons their involvement matters, by communicating with thoughtful intention and respect. Ask if they have any contributions in advance.

- **At least a light agenda.** Design at least a small arc for the flow of the conversation.

- **Know your facilitator.** Who is leading, and what roles do they play?

- **Know your tools.** What technology will help you collect notes and share information?

- **Close with clarity.** Ask for feedback, harvest your takeaways, and decide next steps—while the meeting is still in session.

What if we're in a hybrid situation?

Hybrid = an even bigger lasagne. If some folks are in a physical room, and others are attending virtually, we have to do additional planning, not less. A hybrid environment often looks like a large percentage of people meeting in a physical space, such as a conference room, while additional participants join from home or remote work spaces. Here are a few additional principles to tune into in this situation:

- **Spend additional time on the tech choices.** Zero in on the question of hardware. How will the video and audio be transmitted? How will participants contribute their written digital contributions? How will they see and hear the facilitator and supporting visual assets?

- **Plan for in-person support for technology help.** Ensure there is somebody in the physical room who is able to troubleshoot technical issues. This matters.

- **Ask if the facilitator can stay virtual.** Keeping the role of the facilitator virtual means the facilitator will be oriented towards a mic and video setup that is inclusive for all participants. Ensuring everybody has equal access to an easy-to-see and easy-to-hear facilitator is key.

- **Be aware of accidental exclusions.** When food or additional social interactions are offered to in-person attendees but not to virtual attendees, it creates an inequitable experience for those attending remotely. Instead, be aware of how your agenda and hosting choices can intentionally create inclusion.

We become by doing

We hope that our experiences and tips can help you as you find your own path into becoming the facilitator that only you can be. Facilitation can be a truly transformative and even healing service for a wide array of communities. And, like any potentially healing or transformative service, it can also harm, create distance, or simply be ineffective.

The difference doesn't lie in how perfectly you master any one set of tools and tips, but in how authentically you bring yourself, again and again, to the work of showing up. Of listening. Of building. Of creating and holding space.

It's the resilience to learn and try something new, to be honest enough to voice what is and isn't working, and to be hopeful enough to believe in the work of building, together. Done well, it's a humble yet powerful act of nurturing health for humans in whatever context you find your skills invited into. And to do that, we must nurture health in ourselves first.

Demanding, honest, vulnerable work? Yes. But also worthy, valuable, and critically needed in our time. We are so glad you are joining us on the path of learning.

Resources & templates

Resource

Learning & facilitation readiness assessment

This survey is based on the work of Adrienne maree brown, and is one way to learn about a group's ability to move productively through meetings, workshops and facilitation.

Describing your current reality

The first batch of questions are focused on naming and expressing the problem, as you currently see it.

1. First off, an easy question: what's your name? :)
2. In your own words, what is the "problem" or need you're currently facing?
3. What have you tried already to address this need?
4. If you were to receive external support to address your needs, what outcome would you hope for? (What would success look like for you?)
5. How much time, patience, and commitment does your team have for exploring this problem space?
    a. We are experiencing a great deal of urgency and immediacy, and need short-term help.
    b. We are experiencing the need acutely, but can take our time to address it in a medium-term timeframe.
    c. We are willing to take the time it takes to get to root causes and find healthy solutions.
6. How many participants do you anticipate engaging in this process?

How your group functions in meetings

These questions focus on understanding how your group currently functions in meetings and collaborative spaces.

1. What is the level of connection within this group?
   a. Intimate, familiar (we work and talk together daily)
   b. Professional, regular (we are on the same team)
   c. Active, but not strong (we know each other, but not well)
   d. Distant (we don't work together much, and/or not very effectively)
   e. Strangers (we don't know each other)
2. What is your team's relationship to "joy" in meetings?
   a. We have not felt joyful during and/or after meetings.
   b. We rarely feel joyful during and/or after meetings.
   c. Sometimes we feel joyful during and/or after meetings.
   d. We often feel joyful during and/or after meetings.
3. What is your team's level of vulnerability in meetings?
   a. We have not tried to be vulnerable with each other.
   b. We are rarely vulnerable with each other.
   c. We are sometimes vulnerable with each other.
   d. We are often vulnerable with each other.
4. What level of enrichment do you experience in your meetings?
   a. We have not felt enriched during and/or after meetings.
   b. We rarely feel enriched during and/or after meetings.
   c. Sometimes we feel enriched during and/or after meetings.
   d. We often feel enriched during and/or after meetings.
5. Conflict: when conflict arises, what is the tone in the room?
   a. We're good at conflict: we welcome it, with a solution-oriented mindset.
   b. We're afraid of conflict: we are resistant to name what's going on.
   c. We're unemotional: we push for a quick resolution to conflict, but it doesn't go to the root of the issue.
   d. We avoid conflict: we mentally check out.

e. We're fighters: the tone during conflict is tense and argumentative.

6. How do you move through disagreements?

    a. We struggle to stick to the topic, and we make arguments personal.

    b. We stick to the surface issues, and rush to move things along in ways that leave issues to fester.

    c. We struggle to speak the truth in the room; we have lots of side conversations.

    d. We pay attention to the root systems of the conflict with integrity, and don't waste time.

Do you follow through on tasks and commitments?

1. Yes, we are accountable to each other.
2. No, but we talk about the reasons why.
3. Yes, but with conflict on how the tasks are done, working competitively instead of collaboratively.
4. No, tasks seem to disappear into a black hole.

Are the power dynamics in the room clear? (Who has power? How did they get it?)

1. Yes. The power dynamics are clear and the group is comfortable with them.
2. Not quite—there's a story that the power is shared, but that's not fully true.
3. Yes the power dynamics are clear. But people don't necessarily think it's fair, or know how to change those dynamics.
4. No, the power dynamics are not clear. And the power that is in the room is used to delay action rather than support it.

Would you say all participants would agree on the need to change?

1. Yes, the belief in a need to transform is fully shared.
2. Not quite—we tell ourselves we are in a good state.
3. Yes, we all agree we need change. But folks tend to point the finger at who exactly needs the transformation.
4. No, we do not agree on the need to transform.

Has there been an experience of shared conflict or trauma that you are all working through?

1. Yes, all of us have gone through a shared experience of conflict and trauma, and it has been talked about openly.
2. Yes, we share an experience of conflict or trauma—but it is not talked about openly.
3. No. There has been conflict or trauma, but it has only been experienced by a few individuals.
4. No, we do not recognize having gone through an experience of conflict or trauma.

Is there anything else you'd like to share about this moment for you as a group or individual?

Resource

Chaordic stepping stones

Questions to ask during facilitation discovery, based on original work by Dee Hock

Any discovery process is not just about the information you gather—it's also about the relationship you build. Discovery is about listening, and helping your conversation partner feel heard, seen and known. Therefore, we'd strongly encourage you not to see these as merely survey questions to send, or a form to fill out, but a guide to lead you through a thoughtful conversation. Consider using these prompts in a one-on-one setting, where you connect intentionally with your client, or a workshop where these conversations become a key part of your agenda.

1. Explore the underlying need.

We can open a discovery conversation by working to understand what's going on for folks in their reality. Rather than jumping to prescribed or assumed solutions from either party, we can slow down and build a shared understanding of the current moment. Questions we might ask include:

- What's taking place right now that makes you sense this work is needed?
- What is your sense of what would be most helpful for your current moment?
- If you were to describe the need, as you see it, in your own words, what would you say?
- What can you tell us about the context in which we are operating?
- What do you see in terms of the challenges you are facing?
- What opportunities do you sense you have at this time?

Beyond working to fulfill the organization's goals, you're also working with a human being. What are their needs? You can ask a question like, "What would help you as a person feel like you got what you needed?"

2. Establish a sense of purpose.

Asking about needs might highlight some of the pain and urgency of the "now." But you can also begin tilting towards the hoped-for future outcome by exploring the question of purpose. This has more to do with the "why" of the work. You can try questions like these:

- What is happening that makes this work important for everyone who will participate?
- If we didn't have this [initiative], what would be missed?
- What do we hope this work will do/inspire/create?
- What are the questions at the centre of this work?

3. Create a shared sense of principles.

Before any design choices are made, or any participants are invited, you can begin exploring what type of experience will be meaningful to the participants. This has less to do with what you're accomplishing, and more to do with how the engagement might feel, and what values need to be infused into the work. Questions here might include:

- What is the participant experience we want to create?
- How do we envision people will be interacting and working together during the process?

4. Explore the question of people.

The question of participants in a facilitated encounter matters a lot—who we invite directly influences the work that gets done. Explore the guest list.

- Ask, "Who needs to be in the room?" If you need a prompt, you can think about those who "ARE IN." Those with:

- Authority
- Resources
- Expertise (and lived Experience)
- Information, and
- Need

The work of creating inclusive spaces starts here. Recalling the phrase, "nothing about us, without us, " ask yourself if there are folks who would otherwise simply receive the dictums and output of your work, whose involvement early could make all the difference. You can spur folks on to think a little wider by considering a question like:

- Who might conventionally be left out of conversations like this, but needs to be included?

I also like to understand a little more about what's going on with people before anything is designed. You might go further to ask questions like:

- What can you tell us about the current participants' reality? How are they doing?
- What are they expecting from this experience?

5. Explore the organizing concept.

With the above questions in place, you can begin exploring specific ideas for how the session might come together. Keeping this loose enough to allow continued co-design work matters, but it's important to root all this in what your participants and organizers need, want and expect.

- If we want to meet the need and purpose expressed, the principles discussed, and serve the people mentioned...what sort of concept would work best?
- Generally speaking, what are you sensing the initiative should or could look like (ie, an afternoon workshop, a five-day design sprint, a weekend retreat)? What type of format would work best?
- Can you simplify the format? Do you have a sense of the most basic organizing pattern that would do the job?

6. Open the door to exploring limiting beliefs.

Sometimes, a facilitated experience will run into walls: places where an organization has sacred cows, or areas where participants become unwilling to engage. Being able to surface these early can go a long way towards designing work that is truly effective. However, these questions aren't easy ones to instantly answer. Consider, with a degree of sensitivity, ways you might explore the limiting beliefs present in a culture. You might find questions like this could get you there:

- For this to succeed, is there anything we are sensing we need to let go of?
- What shared beliefs in this culture might block our work together?
- What are you sensing might get in the way?
- In what ways might we be part of the problem?
- Is there anything you're afraid of when you consider this work?
- Can this work enable any new steps forward in your own leadership journey?
- What do you need from your team to feel supported in places of uncertainty?
- Where do you feel your own will is only hesitatingly connected to this project? Where might you be reluctant? What's behind that?

7. Explore the structure needed.

You and your team, client, or organizing partners will need some lightweight parameters for your own work together. Understanding how you'd like to make decisions, share the work, and distribute responsibilities is worth a check.

- How do we want to make decisions? (Are there any rogue voices, undeclared key stakeholders, or other unstated factors that might influence our decision-making?)
- How do we want to organize and coordinate?
- What key roles will be played—and how might you empower the people in those roles?
- What agreements do we need to create to support clarity among

us?

There is no need to over-engineer this. You can be guided by the question, "What is the lightest structure that will serve our purpose and need?"

8. Explore how you'd like to enable a longer-term, sustainable practice.

Workshops, sessions, and collaborative experiences can sometimes feel like a sleep-away camp: an alternative environment is created, far away from everyday life. While this might be magical, it cannot be replicated when we return to our day-to-day routines. In what ways can you set up your one-time facilitated experience to leave a lasting impact once it's done? You can explore questions like:

- Is there anything from the group's current, established ways of working that could work well in this context and be brought into the engagement?
- What can we leverage from our current relationships to get this work done well?
- If we want to sustain this way of working together once it's over, what will we need to consider?
- Are there any commitments that we are willing to make to help this last beyond the short-term?

9. Plan for the harvest.

A good starting point for a discovery process is to build shared expectations for how you'll measure success. What are some ways you can ask about this? You might try questions like:

- What does success look like at the end of this? (Put another way: "Once this session ends, how will you know if it's been a success?")
- Or, zooming out further: "A year from now, what will be different because this experience took place?"

- Or, stated more organizationally: "What are your goals for this work?"

Success in a workshop can be viewed through a harvest metaphor. If seeds are planted, it is with the expectation that fruit will grow. Facilitators sometimes say, "We aren't planning a meeting, we're planning a harvest." So, what do you hope to gather at the end of this? Specifically, you can ask:
- What are the tangible artifacts we want to harvest through this engagement?
- Are there any intangible outcomes we hope to harvest?

From here, the final questions can continue through the co-design phase, and might tend towards the more administrative.
- How many participants do we expect?
- How much time do we have available?
- Are we seeing this happening in-person, virtually, or hybrid?
- Will we need food/snacks/catering for this?
- What sort of supplies do we need? (AV, note-taking, etc.)
- What else do we need to know about the current context for this work? Maybe in your calendar year, your organization life, this current social moment, etc.

Resource

Participant email invitation

Use this template to create a customized invitation for your remote guests.

Subject Line: [Name of Workshop] with [your name / organization name] - Participant Prep Notes!

Body:
Hello there!

On [date] at [time], you are invited to participate in the [name of workshop], facilitated by [facilitator names] from [your organization name]. This is a [X]-hour remote workshop in which [statement of purpose for workshop].

What can you expect from this workshop?

- *Point 1.* And some extra details about it.
- *Point 2.* And some extra details about it.
- *Point 3.* And some extra details about it.

How can you show up best for this workshop?

We have three guiding principles that we'll commit to for the duration of the workshop:

- *Be present.* Turn off distractions (phones, tabs for internet browsing and email checking, other communication notifications). Come on time. Turn on your camera to create a sense of togetherness.

- *Be an active participant.* Our success is dependent on everyone engaging in the work.
- *Be conscious.* Hold space for all team members to contribute. Have an awareness of time, and share the space.

What do you need to do to prepare for this workshop?

Tech set-up

- We'll be using [video platform]! The details of which will be in the calendar invite you received (let me know if you didn't!)
- Grab a pair of headphones (the experience will be better for you and fellow participants!)
- Webcam (it makes such a difference to see your face, and those of other participants)

Environment

- Distraction-free (where possible)
- Prepare some drinks/snacks for the short break times provided

Yourself

- Come with an openness to engage in the process and be present with your team!

If you have any questions leading up to the workshop, please reach out to me!

Looking forward to connecting with you all,
[Your Name]

Resource

Online facilitation: sample workshop agenda flow

We've created this sample agenda with plenty of tips to help you envision and design your own workshop agenda.

In creating a session design, it's an opportunity to take your rough flow and begin getting really specific. However, this comes with a couple important notes, which may seem like paradoxes:

- Yes, the step-by-step sequence of your session design matters a lot.
- But, the goal is never to let the pre-determined schedule completely govern the flow.

Learning to discern what is a valuable use of time is a helpful skill in facilitation. If what emerges in your session deviates from your plan, but truly IS where the participants need to spend time...roll with it! It'll take some experience to get familiar with how long things really take, where you want to be flexible, and where you want to be firm. It's part of what you're developing as a skilled facilitator.

About this template: The times below do not represent an actual workshop, but rather, they are set up to storytell and demonstrate the level of detail one should expect and plan for in a session. It's a sample format for this kind of fine-tuned experience design work.

You can build the same thing in Session Lab, a spreadsheet, blank doc or piece of paper. The key components are:

- Start time of the session
- Name of each activity / block
- Time/length of each activity
- What time it will be on the clock when that activity starts
- Who's facilitating
- Short description or full script for the activity
- Any other key notes / info for you and your co-facilitator

9:00 (15 min)	The welcome and the waiting
9:00 (5 min) Facilitator name	**The waiting** Folks rarely all arrive "on time." Always ensure you've got a buffer planned for late arrivers. - Think through access issues. Virtually, do folks have the right links, software, hardware, connection? On-site, do folks need to shift rooms, find seats, finish a meal? - Think through ambience and atmosphere. During the waiting, should music be playing? In this space, we're thinking through the four As: - Anticipation: Participants arrive knowing what to expect - Access: Accessibility issues are addressed to ensure they can attend - Ambience: The tone is set appropriately - Activation: Participants are about to be called into true work
9:05 (10 min) Facilitator name	**The opening welcome and/or words** What really signifies the start of the session? What is the opening moment? This sets the tone and mood for what's to come. As Priya Parker says, "Never start a funeral with logistics." What's your cue that your experience is about to truly begin?

Your participants are about to enter into their first activity. What needs to be ready before that?
- Do breakout rooms need to be prepared?
- Does a timer need to be ready?
- Are there supplies needed for the activity?

9:15 (30 min)	Activity #1 - Full group dialogue
9:15 (5 min) Facilitator name	**Build in time for instructions and questions** How many minutes does it take for a facilitator to speak out instructions for any activity? How many questions do we anticipate participants will have? A classic mistake new facilitators make is assuming the "time needed for an activity" is the same as "the time an activity will take." Adding a buffer for instructions and questions is good planning.
9:20 (20 min) Facilitator name	**Activity name / description** Some facilitators are comfortable improvising. Others prefer a light outline, and will speak extemporaneously. Still others prefer a precise, specific script, from which they do not deviate. If there is content or instructions for an activity, the opportunity exists to spell it out as specifically as you and your co-facilitators like. **Make sure you consider who's got what.** When working with a co-facilitator, make sure you've clearly assigned sections in advance so you are clear when you're passing the mic, and who's saying what. Consider switching facilitators not after each "block," but rather according to the flow of a session. - For instance, do you want the facilitator who asks the group a question to be the same one to speak back the group's responses, or would it make more sense to switch it up? - Another example: if Facilitator #1 is going to lead a 30-minute interactive Q&A, be ready to pass it over to Facilitator #2 before they pass out from exhaustion.
9:40 (5 min) Facilitator name	**Wrapping up an activity & transitioning** How do you bring a sense of closure to an activity? A short thank you, a brief summary, will often do. How do you transition into the next one? It's as simple as stating "We're now moving into our next activity..."
9:45 (40 min)	Activity #2 - Mentimeter & breakout groups
9:45 (15 min) Facilitator name	**Activity name / description (a sample interactive activity)** Consider diversifying the type of connections you're making by employing short pulse checks, polls or interactive moments. Beyond full-group dialogue, allow folks the chance to reflect as individuals, and contribute their input anonymously. Tools like Mentimeter or Howspace are ideal for this: these are digital platforms that work in hybrid settings too, helping you gather engagement from a screen and fill the room with new meaning.

10:00 (20 min) Facilitator name	**Breakouts** - Full group instructions (1 min) - When in breakouts, sub-facilitators welcome (4 min) - Breakout group conversation (15 min)

About breakout rooms

When we're doing breakout rooms, there are a few things to consider.

- Your instructions: are they clear enough for folks to remember, or written somewhere obvious? Do they know what's expected?
- Do folks understand the time they have available?
- Ideally, you're sending people to breakouts with one job. One task. One question. Don't overcomplicate it. If it's going to get messier than one question, you're going to need to have sub-facilitators helping out in those breakout rooms.
- How are you assigning participants? Are they chosen purposefully in advance, or are they randomly generated on the spot? Have you considered pre-existing power dynamics?

The facilitator's surprise

When breakout rooms are happening—if they are truly participant-driven conversations—this is the moment where you find yourself alone, or with a co-facilitator.

Your first job is to check the clock and make sure you see what's coming around the corner next.

The next job is to get your own immediate needs met: a bio break for yourself, replenishing water or coffee, and getting centered enough to continue.

After those elements, it's often a surprisingly fruitful moment to connect with your co-facilitator, prepare for what's next, or have a moment of genuine conversation.

10:20 (10 min)	**After the breakouts** Coming back from a breakout is a curious moment: folks' energy is activated, perhaps conversations were cut off, perhaps they were really in the zone— or really not connecting at all. Allowing a moment to acknowledge the weirdness before transitioning into the next activity is a welcoming and humane thing to do. It's often valuable to hear a quick report back from what folks covered in their breakout session.
10:30 **(20 min)**	**Break**
10:30 (20 min)	My rule of thumb is to offer a break every 90 minutes --- unless your session is only 90 minutes in the first place! Minds and bodies will return refreshed. This is true especially on screens, but during in-person gatherings, as well. Encourage folks to grab a refreshment, step outside, get some coffee, or take a "bio break".

[Additional activities …]

Time/min: 00:00 (5 min)	**Closing & next steps**

	Don't miss the outro
	Don't let your sessions end with a thud. Orchestrate a thoughtful, curated closing that sends people off on the right note.
	- Logistics:
	  - Do you need to clarify any known follow-up steps?
	  - Do you want to offer an impact survey right away, or will that be sent out later?
	- Group connection:
	  - Are you able to close in a circle or reflection that helps bring home the goals of the session?

By now, you can see this is truly not a real session design. But by the end of your design work, as you manage your timings, your activities, your participant energy, you can also ask yourself:

- What else will we need?
- How are we taking notes?
- Are we needing any unique AV setups?
- If virtual, what about screen sharing, audio sharing, host privileges?
- If in-person, how are our breakout rooms looking? What about snacks, catering, food?

Resource

Basic survey template

Use this template to create your own customized survey for after a workshop or engagement session.

[Your org name] + [Client org name]: [Name of workshop] [Date]

A little feedback goes a long way! Please offer your input on our session together to help us continue to meet our shared aims.

1. Our shared goals for the session were to: [insert your own workshop goals here]. How well did the session meet these goals?

	1	2	3	4	5	
Not very well	O	O	O	O	O	Very well

Let us know what contributed to your rating:

2. Please check all that were true for you in the session (adjust the below as needed to align with your workshop format/content):

- [ ] I felt like my perspectives were incorporated and represented
- [ ] I felt like a psychological safe environment was created
- [ ] I was given adequate time for reflection and thought

☐ I was given opportunities to ask questions
☐ I gained new insights, ideas from the content & frameworks

3. Which content areas of the session were most valuable to you?

	1 - Least valuable	2	3 - Neutral	4	5 - Very valuable
[Insert name of content area 1]	O	O	O	O	O
[Insert name of content area 2]	O	O	O	O	O
[Insert name of content area 3]	O	O	O	O	O
[Insert name of content area 4]	O	O	O	O	O

4. How did the session make you personally, as a participant, feel?

5. What would you hope to explore next with your team in future learning and dialogue?

6. How was your experience with the facilitation overall?

	1	2	3	4	5	
1 star	O	O	O	O	O	5 stars

7. Any final feedback to share about the facilitation in general — hosting, session design, and technology choice?

Resource

The online facilitation checklist

Here's our handy checklist for planning a successful online facilitation experience.

Pre-event

☐ **Establish a purpose**

Why are we meeting? What is this gathering going to do?

☐ **Build alignment between participants**

Have any proactive one-on-one conversations that might be necessary.

☐ **Invite with intention**

Send an invitation (email or other) that opens with the purpose of the event (what it is and why it matters) and how attendees are invited to show up and participate. Include logistical details at the end:

- Date and time
- The technology (meeting platform, additional tools)

☐ **Design the agenda**

☐ **Establish roles**

- Content Facilitator
- Technical Facilitator
- Technical Producer

☐ **Select the technology**

During event

☐ **Set your workspace up for success**
- Have a second monitor.
- Ensure easy access to all tools, agendas, communication channels.

☐ **Lead with presence**

Post-event

☐ **Ask for feedback**
   Create and send out a survey for participants.

☐ **Harvest takeaways**
- What was generated from the workshop?
- What are the next steps?

Resource

Recommended online tools

While we use a wide variety of online tools, a couple stand out as worth passing along.

Miro

miro.com
An intuitive online whiteboard for easy digital collaboration.

Session Lab

Sessionlab.com
A platform that provides powerful workshop agenda design and collaboration support.

We partner with Crewjoy

crewjoy.com
An online team-strengthening app that helps individuals share their work needs, styles and preferences with each other.

Manufactured by Amazon.ca
Bolton, ON

34342430R00055